Going Beyond

Going Beyond

Dr. Krupa Sindhu Nayak

Translated by
Pareswar Biswal

With a Foreword by
Prof. Bhagaban Jayasingh

BLACK EAGLE BOOKS
Dublin, USA | Bhubaneswar, India

Black Eagle Books
USA address:
7464 Wisdom Lane
Dublin, OH 43016

India address:
E/312, Trident Galaxy, Kalinga Nagar,
Bhubaneswar-751003, Odisha, India

E-mail: info@blackeaglebooks.org
Website: www.blackeaglebooks.org

First International Edition Published by
Black Eagle Books, 2023

GOING BEYOND
by **Dr. Krupa Sindhu Nayak**

Translated by **Pareswar Biswal**

Original Copyright © Dr. Krupa Sindhu Nayak
Translation Copyright © Pareswar Biswal

All rights reserved. No part of this publication may be reproduced, stored in a retrieval system, or transmitted, in any form or by any means, electronic, mechanical, photocopying, recording or otherwise without the prior permission of the publisher.

Cover photography: **Tan.**
Interior Design: Ezy's Publication

ISBN- 978-1-64560-350-4 (Paperback)
Library of Congress Control Number: 2023932414

Printed in the United States of America

To my daughter Leeza,
son-in-law Satyen,
son Shreetam and
daughter-in-law Komal
who have always understood
and appreciated my concerns and
have encouraged me to pursue them.

CONTENTS

Foreword	09
Translator's Note	11
Preface	17
The Muses' Message	25
Time to Ponder	27
Reiteration	32
The Gentleman	37
Going Beyond	40
Poetry Gone in Vain	43
Stars in the Night Sky	48
Incarnation	51
The Homecoming Message	55
Life As It Is	58
Transcendence	61
Memories of the Monsoon	65
The Flux	69
A Portrait of the Twenty-first Century	74
Under the Shade of a Fruit-bearing Tree	78
The Parting Moment	81
The Forgotten Destination	84
A Different place : A Different Awakening	88

Foreword

Dr Krupa Sindhu Nayak has been one of the most prolific poets of Odisha who emerged on the literary scene in the early 1970s. A surgeon by profession, he has authored seven collections of poetry, including *Baya Chadheira Dukha*, 2007 (Woes of the Weaver Bird), his magnum opus, besides eleven plays, and several short stories which he has turned into stage and radio plays.

His poetry, as I understand, explores deeper and more profound topics such as life, death, time, and more importantly his place and identity in this chaotic and disconnected universe. The experience of modern man as something shocking and of distressful consequences finds adequate representation in his poetry of the 90s and after. He used dark imagery to vindicate his position in situations which are otherwise cruel and hostile to man's survival on this earth. This is where he compared life on the earth to a "hanging nest," a kind of "prison cell," where man is kept as "a prisoner" in the horrifying "darkness" of "unending woe."

But in his later poetry Dr. Nayak abandoned much of complexity, disillusionment and difficulty in expression of his early years in favour of love, happiness, love of nature, and reminiscences of the past and memory. His poetry began to embrace romantic strain and nostalgia, and a new technique to express ordinary events of life.

Going Beyond, as the title suggests, talks about the poet's attempt to transcend his existence or experience beyond the physical level. The transcendence he longs for in the midst of the din and bustle of modern life is not easy to achieve as he is not able to "renew my bonds" with the ultimate reality. It is like "failing" to recall the "lines that aspire/to go beyond the words."

Dr Nayak is admired for the way he plays with words, particularly when he fishes out the recollections of the past; it might be his days when the monsoon rain had ravaged his village with a deluge, or the village which in some other time had turned "bald and barren", with the "groves and orchards," losing their "greenery." He also celebrates his memory of Katpadi on his way to CMC Hospital, Vellore, where he was doing residency in surgery in the early 70s. It is heartening to note how the interior architecture of his memories and recollections forms the still centre of his art of this period. His dexterous use of imagery aims at startling the reader by expressing the mood of his poetic persona or temper of the age.

Going Beyond reaffirms Dr Nayak's position as a progressive humanist, and this volume can be taken as an open sesame to the beautiful world of the poet's experience which the readers must share as their own and feel the thrill of pleasure that good poetry always offers.

I am sure *Going Beyond* will become a great success.

Prof. Bhagaban Jayasingh
Professor and Dean
School of Communication
ASBM University, Bhubaneswar

Translator's Note

Originally published in Odia a few years ago (2016), titled **'Atikraman'**, this volume by Dr. Krupa Sindhu Nayak, a noted Odia poet, contains eighteen poems. When I read it for the first time, what struck me instantly was its simplicity and straightforwardness: simplicity of style and diction and straightforwardness in expression. I also noticed that it heralded a marked departure from his earlier works, departure both in intent and in content. If his concerns in his earlier works, especially in his 'Baya Chadheira Dukha' (Sorrows of the the Weaver Bird) were largely philosophical, here in this volume, they are patently sociopolitical. Perhaps, this departure is a conscious and deliberate act. Having spent a lifetime indulging his passion for poetry, he now realizes that all his efforts have gone in vain :

> So poetry remained
> Where it was –
> between the covers
> of impressive volumes
> stacked on the shelves
> unopened, unread
> And uncared for
> *(Poetry Gone in Vain)*

Thus the mood now is one of self-doubt :
> Could I have
> brought a beautiful dawn
> To the horizon
> I have spent a lifetime
> painting with
> the colours of my words ?
>
> *(Life As It Is)*

And the mood is so poignant that it borders on self-pity :
> Alas, my empathetic recreation
> of their world
> went in vain,
> for, my pen could
> never approach their pain ;
>
> *(Life As It Is)*

The 'they' that the poet is so concerned about in this volume are the toiling masses, and he is acutely conscious of the fact that he has hardly been able to make any difference to their lives :
> And for those
> whose voice poetry could have been,
> the long night continues
> without an end
> and the agonized cries of the earth
> die down
> around the bend.
>
> *(Life As It Is)*

Though the theme of each poem in this volume is different from the other's, the common thread that binds them together is this overwhelming consciousness of personal and collective failure, the failure to secure a just and equitable social order. Hence, the mood is one of guilt, regret and self-pity that borders almost on self-recrimination.

The utterances throughout the volume are so sincere and so heart-felt that it is difficult to separate the poet from the poetic persona (the narrator). In fact, there are a few narrative poems where the narrator is palpably the poet himself. Sample this :

Years ago
I left my childhood days behind
in my village;
they would not return
like the monsoon every year
or ever.
But every time I get drenched
in the early monsoon shower,
I go back to those
unforgettable days
soaking in the rustic romance
of every sweet hour.
(Memories of the Monsoon)

There are a few poems in this volume on personalities and recollections *(Incarnation, Under the Shade of a Fruit-bearing Tree, The Forgotten Destination, A Different Place : A Different Awakening).* They too are saturated with the same overarching sentiments of universal love and sympathy.

Dr. Naik's poetry has always been marked by its lack of intellectual pretensions. The allusions and references in his works are so familiar and the poetic devices like similes, metaphors and images are so rooted in the native soil that any ordinary reader in the Odia language can instantly relate to them. These aspects of his poetry are more pronounced in this volume as he makes a conscious effort to address a larger audience. His target audience here is not the cognoscenti, but the common man.

Therefore, I felt this volume deserves the attention of a world-wide readership. Hence, this translation.

But before I sat down to translate it, I recalled that I had once stumbled upon an online article by a fellow-translator who, while describing his own experience, observed that the very act of translation is 'soul crushing'. Another practitioner of the same trade, in response, called it just the opposite: 'exhilarating'. It was immediately obvious to me that they were both right. Yet their assessments of their experiences differed so drastically because they were looking at two different aspects of the same preoccupation : the process and the product. I fully empathise with the former as I have gone through the same 'soul crushing' process every time I have sat down to translate something; only, I would rather describe it as 'brain wracking' instead of 'soul crushing'. Even while reading the source text for the first time, I have gone through the torturous process of looking for what Eugene Nida calls 'dynamic equivalence' in the target language. And I also share in the 'exhilarating' feelings of the latter as I have felt like exclaiming with a 'eureka' every time I have found it.

If the translator's preoccupation is with poetry, these two opposing emotions are further heightened as finding the perfect equivalence for a word, a phrase, an idiom or a reference is a still more arduous task; and even if one finds it, it may not fit into the rhythm of the line, the structure of the stanza, the cultural construct of the emotion conveyed or the overall framework of the poem. Thus, the translator has to look for an alternative one. Perhaps that is primarily the reason why translation is called transcreation and the translator's job as a transcreator is to maintain a perfect balance between being faithful to the source text and transforming it into an independently aesthetic end-product in the target language.

I have sincerely tried to follow these principles while translating this volume. I have retained certain typical Odia words and expressions as they are in the source text wherever I have found the equivalence inadequate or where I have felt it necessary to retain them for the sake of maintaining the original charm, of course, with footnotes wherever necessary. Explanatory footnotes have also been given for events, occasions, personalities and allusions which are typical to Odishan history, culture, literature and folklore.

On occasions, though rare, I have consciously borrowed with quotation marks words and phrases from well-known English poems where strikingly similar sentiments have been sought to be conveyed in the source text.

Pareswar Biswal

Preface

Time to Make the World a Bit More Beautiful

The urban man
has lost everything
Preoccupied with his profession
busy in building
his children's career
furiously tapping away
on his laptop in the office
or at home
chatting with his friends
on Whatsapp
or making new friends
on Facebook,
he hasn't kept count
of how many he has lost
at the club, at the seminar
or while having fun
at the party.

Does he know
where he is now ?
And where are those
who once mattered
so much to him ?
How should he ?

He wasn't even aware
when the ground
under his feet gave way.

While blindly running
the race towards
an imaginary peak,
he had no time
to pause and ponder
if he had not lost his way
in the wilderness,
and to wonder
if he was running
towards his destination
or had taken a road
in the opposite direction.

Weary and tired of
running an unending race
he now looks back
to find his best years
behind him
and for the rest
of his life
he tries his best
to wean his
grand children away from TV
to make them listen
to his stories of success
of how hard he worked
to reach the peak
of his career
how meticulously

he built
a beautiful house
for himself
and his family;
and how interesting
his experiences were
on his foreign trips.

As he goes on and on
it never occurs to him
what he would say
if someone asked him -
All that is alright,
but have you ever
stopped on your way
to pick up a wounded bird
writhing in pain
under a tree
to offer it a drop of water
and the balm
of a fond caress ?

Or have you ever
halted for a while
to look at
the shelterless man
lying on the pavement
shivering in the cold
and to offer
him a cover ?
Or have you ever
rejoiced in
somebody else's success?

Have you ever
missed the thrills and throes
of your childhood
while enjoying
the orchestra at the City Centre
during the *Raja*[1] festival?

While telling
sundry such tales
of his weather-beaten sagacity
he never bothered
about what to say
if one asked him why
the world now looks uglier
than it was ever before
and why every time
one steps out
into the market,
the hotel, the hospital
or even to the temple,
one faces everywhere
the same spider web
of doubt and fear.

And why
in the suburban slums
one hears
again and again
the same cries
of hungry children.

---

1   *A popular festival in coastal Odisha heralding the onset of the monsoon.*

Have you ever
been moved by those cries
or did you have
only a lump of palpitating flesh
where your heart
ought to have been?

And can you tell us
why the faint trickle
of human suffering
of your times
has now turned
into such a terrible deluge ?

Isn't it time
you wondered why
you found it so hard
to call your unfortunate neighbour 'brother'
while you gladly sang
paeans to the glory
of an ephemeral motherland;
and why you
could not invite
the *'Chandaluni'*[2] to your home
though you earned
all the plaudits
for having dinner
at her place ?

---

2   A 'dalit woman'; an obvious allusion to *'Sriya Chandaluni'* of *Laxmi Puran,* an Odia classic of the early sixteenth century by Balaram Das. The poet attempted to establish a casteless society of universal equality through this work.

The world is one family -
we have been told
ever so many times;
yet why do we have
so many walls
dividing us
into little ghettos ?
Why do we live
In perennial fear
Of one another ?
Why this sabre-rattling
these war cries
and the mad race
to acquire the thunder ?

Isn't it time
we got out of the labyrinth
of our manufactured fears
and rose above the walls
to make the world
a bit more beautiful
in our lifetime ?
We have somehow
managed to live
our lives
under the shadow of fears.

Can't we now
hope to bequeath
our children
a world where
they can move about
freely and without fear

where they can
live happily
ever after ?

This small question
has ever so greatly
agitated me
and has been
the source and inspiration
of all my poems.

Krupa Sindhu Nayak

The Muses' Message

Is poetry
a unique sublimation
of pent up feelings
from the depth
of the heart
or the downpour
of divine inspirations ?

But surely
poetry does not
belong to heaven.
It is nothing more than
an unending earthly quest
for an evolved life
free from the shackles
of self-doubt
suffering and incertitude.

Is poetry
merely a procession of words
or as someone said –
'the best words
in the best order'?
It is rather
the combined echo
of words and their interplay
like the one that

comes back to you
in waves from within a cave
to awaken you
from your slumber
to arouse your conscience
or just to liven up
your spirit.

Like the sunlight trying hard
to pierce through
the rainforests
to brighten up the path
in the wilderness,
poetry has striven
down the ages
to lead light
'amidst the encircling gloom',
'over the moor and fen'
of ignorance and the
'crag and torrent'
of inhumanity.

The meaning of poetry
lies beyond the words,
in the songs
of the Muses
as they happily sing
their benevolent tidings
with the pitter-patter
of the rain-drops
while the clouds
descend from heaven
onto the earth.
▫▫

Time to Ponder

Sometimes, some stars
look brighter than the others
and volumes of sparkling poetry
are written on them;
but are they good enough
to show us the way ?

Some of those poems
look like a woman
just stepping out
of a beauty parlour
after an intensive session
of facial and manicure;
but their cosmetic romance
hardly allows one
to make with them
much headway.

A king once
was divinely ordered
in his dream
to build a splendid temple
and install in it
an image of a deity
to restore order
to his chaotic kingdom.

He did likewise
and his subjects
devoutly flocked at the temple
to pray to the god
to deliver them
from droughts, hunger and scarcity.

They were happy
to receive their provisions
from the royal stores;
they flocked at
the temple more and more
singing paeans to
the glory of the god
and to that of
their earthly lord.

The king felt
he had won a war
by winning
the unruly mob over.
At last he heaved
a sigh of relief
assured that his
flocks were happy
with their belief.

The king rewarded
the ministers
for their loyal
services rendered
and enjoyed his time
in the harem

without a care
in the world;
his courtiers too
had a holiday
they thought
they had long deserved.

He went on
to invade
the neighbouring kingdoms
whenever he so desired
while his admirers
stood in awe
of his charisma
and merrily applauded.

The grovellers
garnered all the medals,
The bootlickers
all the bounties
as the poets
the artists and the wise
remained silent by-standers;
the loyal subjects
soon realized
that their fate
was written in stone
and they rose
in revolt again.

Certain things did change
as a result
the set, the players

and the rule of the game;
a new set of dealers
replaced the old one
and opened the stores
to the flocks once again.
The king and his courtiers
masked themselves
to reappear as frontmen
for the masses;
the republic
with daily doles
bought the public over
and kleptocracy reigned supreme
while the republican
flag fluttered overhead.

They shone brighter
than ever before
in the panegyrics
of their flunkeys and minions;
and some of them
got so drunk
on their new-found clout
that they made
an ass of the law
to freely move
in the orbits
of their shenanigans.

The best sold
themselves away
while the worst
chose to beg their way;

and like the drop
in the value of all values
the value of the rupee
fell to one and half-penny
we did not know
power had undone so many.

But we can now hear
the raucous war cry
of the restless youth
echoing like a distant thunder
and the wise
are beginning to
rise from their slumber.

Look ! The eastern sky
is brightening up
and the dawn
of good days
may not be far away.

☐☐

Reiteration

Who knew
such an unthinkable
would ever happen ?
That the history
of mankind would
someday take such a turn
to veer away
from the syncretic way
shown by the sages
to descend into
the narrow, divided
domain of selfish men ?

Despite the unwavering faith
and devout prayers
and worships for ages,
the gods and goddesses
never deigned
to step down
from their pedestals
nor did they ever
walk out of their images
to bless the suffering masses
with good health and wealth.

Neither the brutish
instincts of man
were defeated
nor was the promised land
of truth and justice
of the sages' sermons
delivered.

Hence they ushered in
the lofty ideals of
equity and fraternity
that soon lost their way
in the vortex of
personal ambitions
of powerful men.

The fustian principles
were soon consumed
by the insatiable desires
of hungry men;
the stream of compassion
lost its way
in the desert sand
and what was
left of it
was a dead river.

Myriads of false promises
Flowed like a deluge
and flashed like
dazzling mirages
in that river,
vote-banks were built

on the sands of
those empty promises
like the toy towers
of children's games;
and the fate of the nation
hung in the balance
of the fixed deposits
of those promises.

The bulldozers of progress
soon rolled down
into the forests;
the greenery of
the forest land
was burnt down
in the all-engulfing
fire of man's greed
for more and more
and the wild animals
looking for a habitat
are now invading
the concrete jungles
where their beastly nature
is beaten by
still more bestial acts
of rape, riot, murder
extortion and plunder,
where the age-old
values of love, compassion
and humanism
bereft of their meanings
are now stacked
on the racks of

libraries and museums;
and where crooks and criminals
work their way
to amass millions
to be declaimed against
and punished
only on the pages of fiction
or on the frames
of feature films.

The wise have been enslaved
and the poets
have retired to their cosy clubs.
The law is an ass
which the mightly
can beat
to suit their selfish ends.

Now is the time
to fight that enemy
and banish its deadly ghost
from your system
to free yourself
from the shackles of selfishness
and restore the order
of the universe.

The order that makes
the planets
move in their orbits
and ordains the wind
and the clouds
to serve the eternal will.

Now is the time
to open your window
to have a fresh look
at the horizon
and to hear
the message of poetry
even at the cost
of a repetition.

◻◻

The Gentleman

Ignoring the calls
of a greater life
he spent his best years
in pursuit of
his own advancement.

He never had the time
to bother about
the causes and effects
of things
nor did he have
the inclination
to look for the symptoms
of the malaise
and find a remedy.

He chose not to remember
those who gave him
birth, upbringing and education;
and like a farmer
busy harvesting the crops
turning his back on
the bare parched fields,
he turned a blind eye
to the poverty

of his people
while chasing the dreams
of his own prosperity.

And now
in the autumn of his life
as he looks back on
the years gone by
the splendor of his living room
displaying his achievements
and the impressive
array of his acquisitions
now feels like
a deadweight upon his chest.

The number of protesting voices
he had willfully suppressed
within himself
far outweigh
the amounts of favour
he had obsequiously received.

His contrite soul
now wonders
why like a lone
palm tree in a desert
helplessly weathering the sandstorm,
he kept quiet
when he was
expected to speak out
and why
he slunk away
like a slithering creature

when he ought to have
stood firm and straight.

And how,
tied all his life
to his family, occupation
and the vagaries
of the market,
counting the losses and gains
on the bonds
of his mutual funds,
he lived a worthless life
that could have
come to greater use.

Is it not his fault
that ruthlessly manipulating hawks
have taken over the palace
and every inch of the space
he quietly conceded
while the suffering masses
were still bleeding
through their primitive wounds ?

His could have been
the voice they needed
to deliver them
from the prayer books.
Pity, he wasted
more than half a century
preferring to steer
the middle course.

Going Beyond

Like a mountain spring
cutting its way
through the crags,
life, ever since it
appeared on planet earth,
has fought its way
through the apparently
insurmountable hurdles
as naturally as
the moon passes through the clouds
and the clusters of stars.

It has gone on
and gone beyond
as spontaneously
as the whirlwind
rising in a sudden gust
snatches away
the scarf from a woman's shoulder
without shaking
a leaf on the tree,
and as imperiously
as an express train
whistles through the hills and dales.

It has dealt with
umpteen challenges
of infancy, adolescence
and youth
at times merrily
and at times stoically
and has taken
everything in its stride
like a student
anxiously preparing
for a crucial test
or like a would be mother
going through the pangs
of childbirth.

Sometimes it has lost
a game on the cusp of a win
and sometimes
snatched a win
from the jaws of defeat.

Unexpected setbacks
suffered like
a bolt from the blue,
actions that have
led to unforeseen consequences-
all come within
the ambit of its karma.

Dark nights with their
horrible nightmares
come and go
daybreak soon

leads to the noon;
the sum total of
successes and failures
seems like the cargo
carried away
by the evening train.

Some wounds
heal up in time
the search for the remedy
of those that do not
is still on;
the boatman
has not given up hope
against the sweep
of the storm.

The ebb and flow
of life
but teaches us
one lesson
that the mighty
have taken over
the world by birth;
the meek can hope
that some day they will
inherit the earth.

☐☐

Poetry Gone in Vain

Like an old-world
oriental bride
poetry has remained
behind the veils
since the ancient times.

Her message has been lost
in the wilderness
like the fragrance
of sweet-smelling flowers
in a blizzard,
for those whose cause
she intended to take up
either misunderstood
her bleeding heart
or did not understand
it at all.

Yet like the sun
struggling through dark clouds
she incessantly strove
to reach their hearts;
embellished herself
with countless
newly-fashioned ornaments.
But no one

opened their doors
to welcome her;
no one thought it fit
to have a word with her.

She thought she had
something to say
and she hoped
she could show them the way.
But they were too busy
building mansions
for their masters
and too worried about
finding their next meal
of greens and watered-rice
to find time
for the luxury
of her gilt-edged gifts.

High on their
bowls of *handia*[1]
they spent
dreamless nights
deep in slumber
in their slums.

Poetry repelled them
like the text-books
of poetry did
repel their school-going children;
perhaps they thought

---

[1] *A cheap country liquor of fermented boiled rice, a favourite with the tribals of Odisha.*

it was meant for
their children
to deal with
in the exam papers.

And those who fed and fattened
on their sweat and blood
secretly amassed
their surplus wealth
in foreign banks;
they too turned away
from her
for fear
she might show
them the mirror
and bite their
guilt-ridden conscience
in their solitary hours.

Had the toiling masses
listened to her
they could have found
a resonance
in their hearts
to prevent the offshoots
of hunger and terror.

And those who
came to occupy
positions of power
by fair means or foul,
blared their hearts out
in praise of the poets

on public platforms;
the acknowledged legislators
often quoted
one of them
to call them
the unacknowledged legislators
felicitated them
with plaques and shawls.

But when it was time
for a line of poetry,
they ran away
on the pretext
of their busy schedule
to receive
rousing welcomes
from their loyal lackeys
waiting for them
at another platform.

Those who were
left in between –
the so-called thinkers
and intellectuals-
were busy writing
weekly columns
or paneling paid TV debates;
they too had
no time for poetry
except to occasionally quote
an odd oft-quoted line
to earn browny points.

So poetry remained
where it was –
between the covers
of impressive volumes
stacked on the shelves
unopened, unread
and uncared for,
yet the poets
continued to pride themselves
upon their plaques
panegyrics and pittances.

◻◻

Stars in the Night Sky

When one comes back home
after a foreign tour,
especially of the west,
one feels the difference
between this country
and those
one visited;
the difference between
light and darkness,
between common sense
and ignorance.

What is the source
of the darkness
that we in this land
are still groping through ?
Is it our prehistoric atavism
that takes us back
into the caves
again and again
and leaves us riven
by caste, creed
community and religion ?

Splattered with blood
of hatred and terror

this accursed land
is confronted with
fear and danger.

We hoped for
an evolved life
and fondly believed
that the liberal
republican spirit of the nation
would reform them.
Good shall prevail
over evil, we were told;
we had waited for ages
and were willing to wait
till the end of the world.

Evolve they did
and morphed into
self-seeking politicos
in a new set-up.
They said they were there
to serve the masses
and serve they did well
but only themselves
after they plunged into
the electoral power-game
as naturally as
buffaloes in summer
take to slimy pools.

They called it
the age of the republic
and launched

the phase of progress
with much fanfare;
their vote-banks
soon led them the way
to the Swiss Bank
as the wise quietly
watched the plight
of their denuded motherland
like their forefathers did
while Draupadi
was being stripped
of her clothes.

The stars in the night sky
still glittered
as the world around them
remained enveloped
in darkness
while the hungry
and the hopeless
groped for a ray of hope.

Yet we can hear
the rumbles within
heralding the beginning
of the war
and that gives us the hope
that the dark night
is about to end
and that the impending war
can be won.

❐❐

Incarnation

The countrymen waited
long for a messiah
to descend from heaven
and to save them
from the jaws
of hungry crocodiles
who masqueraded
as their saviors;
for,
more than half a century's
belied hopes
had taught them
to know the thugs
by their masks.

For long
the crocodiles shed
their false tears
from umpteen platforms
while their victims
caught between their jaws
hopelessly cried
for help.

He came
not descending from heaven

in celestial splendor
nor charioted and heralded
by gods and goddesses
but walking down
the country side
in his ordinary dhoti-kurta
and a Gandhi cap –
a largely featureless
short-statured man
with no pretensions
to being an avatar.

He came
with no flag, no fanfare
and no following;
he did not lead
raucous rallies
nor did he give
rousing speeches.

Like his guru
who once dreamt of
the *Ram Rajya*[2],
he straighaway sat
on a fast-onto-death
to rediscover
the powers of *satyagraha*[3]
and unleashed
an earthquake
that soon shook
the well-entrenched pillars

---

2   *Utopia, the ideal world that Gandhi dreamed of.*
3   *Gandhi's method of passive resistance.*

of chicanery and corruption.
He soon turned into an icon
for the masses
as his message spread
far and wide
like wild fire
and took in its sweep
the entire nation.
The self-proclaimed guardians
of the masses
hurriedly tried
their scurrilous methods
to protect their vested interests
though many of them
scurried for cover.

Sadly, some of them,
believing that
nothing had happened
and nothing had changed,
kept themselves busy
cultivating their vote-banks
in preparation for
the next election.

His love for his
country and countrymen
was the spark
the masses needed.
It is now upto them
to feel the depth
of his words and deeds
and to keep the flame alive.

He though is determined
to be the last man standing
fighting on their behalf
till his last breath.

❐❐

(Upon Anna Hazare's launch of the 'India-against-Corruption' movement)

The Homecoming Message

Like a flock of birds
that never found a nest
nor even a cage
for themselves
and for long
aimlessly flapped around
in the wilderness of the sky,
they suddenly swooped down
upon their tormentors
to reclaim their habitat.

As the message
of the uprising spread
far and wide,
those who were breathless
under the jackboots
of their assailants
came out of their holes
like hordes of snakes
and fell upon them
to bite them hard
in vengeance.

A long, protracted
and bloody battle ensued
before the flag of freedom

finally fluttered
over their head
upon the blood and sweat
of the dead.

And now
seven decades later
the weather-beaten flag,
tattered and bereft of
its lofty goals
of equity, fraternity and prosperity,
still flutters
long after its sheen
has melted into thin air
like the grey chimney smoke;
and long after
its three colours have faded
under the pretentious platitudes
of manipulating politicos.

It still flutters
long after the deluge
of developmental promises
lost its way
somewhere between
the capital and the countryside.

And those in the slums,
in the villages
and in the depths of the forests
who once looked at it
with hope and expectations
waited for years

before they left
when the bulldozers
of growth and progress
arrived to mow down
their shacks and shanties.

The capital city
in the meanwhile
has marched ahead
and has grown
by leaps and bounds
with its malls and multiplexes
and corporate towers
towering over
the small aspirations
of countless souls in the crowd
and covering their putrid corpses
with a sleek shroud.

The other day,
heard someone in the crowd say –
It is time
the veneer of progress
and its sham slogans
were removed;
it is time
the message of the tricolor
was reclaimed.

☐☐

Life As It Is

For years
their sweat and tears
have agitated me;
their hunger, poverty
and haplessness
have troubled my conscience.
And I have always hoped
that I will find
a way out for them
only if I could
make their suffering mine.

Often I have wondered
if I could have helped
the storm-beaten birds
regain their flight
or at least
could have put them
back in their nests;
and if I could have
offered a piece of cover
to the half-naked man
lying under
the roadside tree
shivering in the cold
on a chilly night.

Could I have
brought a beautiful dawn
to the horizon
I have spent a life time
painting with
the colours of my words ?

And could I have touched
the borders of their consciousness
with my self-deluding
depths of experience ?

I thought I could relive their plights
on the pages of my poetry
and show them the mirror
from the depths of my heart.

Alas, my empathetic recreation
of their world
went in vain
for my pen could
never approach their pain;
happy as they were
with the dole of
a bowl of rice for rupees two,
they had no time
for my meticulously built
world of words.

They are still lotus-eating--
my fellow poets;
writing poetry for its sake
or for the sake

of their own pleasure.
They too have no time
to look at the mirror images
of their words.

And for those
whose voice poetry could have been,
the long night continues
without an end
and the agonized cries of the earth
die down
in the primordial darkness
around the bend.

◻◻

Transcendence

I was sitting
alone in the train
waiting for the next station
while my fellow-passengers
had gone asleep.

The whiste of the train
that mingled with their snores
gradually weakened
and I knew
I was approaching
Katpadi station
that was so dear to my heart.

I peeped through the windows
and saw the rows
of street lights
twinkling at a distance
as though the sky
had descended
upon the city of Vellore
with all her stars.

Sadly, I was passing by
the same city
and could not revisit it

to renew my bonds
and to refresh the myriad memories
etched in my mind for years.

I wished I could –
as I used to –
take a rickshaw
from the station
upto the CMC[4]
where I spent
a greater part of my best years
curing the wounds
and sharing in the sufferings
of so many unknown souls.

I have stepped on to
the platform so many times
wishing to relive those happy days
at my dear old CMC;
but every time
I have passed by
Leaving it to another day.

The train soon
stopped at Katpadi
and I eagerly stepped out
to have a look around;
the platform had changed
so much in the meantime
I could not find
a trace of the old one.

---

4   *Christian Medical College, Vellore, India*

I walked upto
my favourite bookstall
but the face at the counter
appeared unknown;
I tried to recall
the name of the one I knew
but failed
just as I have failed
so may times
with the names of
my old school-mates.

The whistle of the train
brought me back
into the compartment
and amidst the snores
of my fellow-passengers
I went upto my berth
with a hollowness
in my heart
wondering if I would
ever have another chance
if time would erase
all those sweet memories
or if I could keep them alive
in the lines of my poetry –
lines that aspire
to go beyond the words.

I soon felt sleepy
and in that drowsy hour
I could hear
a cry from CMC's

surgical wards
and someone calling me
waving his hands
from the rooftops
of its residents' quarters.

□□

Memories of the Monsoon

Years ago
I left my childhood days behind
in my village;
they would not return
like the monsoon every year
or ever.
But every time I get drenched
in the early monsoon shower,
I go back to those
unforgettable days
soaking in the rustic romance
of every sweet hour.

The cool breeze of the monsoon
finds me everywhere
sneaking into my bedroom
at the most unearthly hour
following me into my office,
hospital, lecture hall,
at times to a different city
or even to a foreign land
like a besotted lover.

I remember
how one particular year
the monsoon clouds broke loose

to cause a vast deluge
when the river
swelled overnight
and broke through the embankments.

Vast stretches of land
remained submerged for days
and people along with
their children and livestock
were ferried across
in country-boats
and on bamboo-floats
to seek shelter
under make-shift structures
and tent houses
raised on the mounds
and the high points of the river banks.

They lay there
marooned, starving
eagerly waiting for
a *Gopabandhu*[5]
to arrive with food packs
and relief materials.

The ministers and government officials
had an aerial view
from their helicopters
and by the time
they dropped food packs
too little, too late

---

5 Utkalmani Gopabandhu Das, the legendary philanthropist and freedom fighter of the early twentieth century Odisha.

many were dead
and many were still dying
of cholera, of influenza
or from sheer starvation.

And those who survived
came back home
to pick up the threads
of their tattered lives
and to start everything
from the scratch.

The monsoon has grown
fickle over the years
suddenly pouring down
at some places
sweeping away villages
waterlogging cities
disrupting transport
and communication
while forgetting
to visit the places
where it is
needed the most.

Those who are affected
look to the skies
hoping for happy tides
from the rain gods;
and those who are not
smugly watch TV debates
and uproars in the parliament
over the drought, the deluge

and the incidents
of farmers' suicide.

The government machinery
swings into action
under media pressure;
money flows
in a spate of activities
and lands in the hands
of crooks
while the fate of the victims
and the whims of the monsoon
remain unchanged.

Rains and the monsoon
have parted ways of late;
rain-clouds have forgotten
the address of their destination.
The cool breeze has turned hot
under the ruthless sun;
the humidity is unbearable
with the frequent power-cuts
during the endless dry spells.

Like an unfaithful lover
the monsoon has lost
its charms of romance
and its memories
of the by-gone days
now look like
the relics of another age.

☐☐

The Flux

Whenever I go
to the bank of the river Koel
and spend an odd hour
sitting there,
I feel like
diving into the water
and swim across
to the other side
as I used to do
in the company of my school friends
during the long summer days.

We would swim
with the current for hours
at times just keeping afloat
and letting ourselves
flow down the stream
till we touched
the bank on the other side
at a bend.

A lot of water
has flowed down the river
ever since I left my village
and my mother's
tearful eyes behind

not knowing that
I was snapping
the bond forever.

The bond snapped further
little by little every year
as batches of young men
left the village
year after year
like the river in spate
nibbling at it
with her landslides
and like the greenery
around the village
losing a part of it
with the tropical cyclones
slashing through every summer.

Yet we occasionally
returned to our village
during the *Puja*[6] holidays
or summer vacations
trying to renew our ties
as best as we could.
But our children
busy with their coaching classes
and entrance tests
hardly had time
for such sentiments;

---

6   *Durga Puja, celebrated in honour of goddess Durga as a symbol of the triumph of good over evil.*

city-bred as they were
they had no umbilical connection
with the land of their
fathers and forefathers.

Growing up on a diet
of chow mein, pizza, manturian
and assorted items of
McDonald's fast food,
they had no taste
for the home-made country cakes
of rice and molasses
our mothers occasionally sent us.

They had their
campus selections
before they had
completed their education;
they took leave
of their parents and well-wishers
before boarding the planes or trains.
Did they know
they were taking leave
from the hearts
of their mothers
and motherland forever ?

And those who were left behind
hated the mud and slush
of their farmland;
some of them left for the cities
to somehow make a living;

some others
wimpishly approached the politicos
to curry favour with them
and were happy
to be hired and carried
to the capital city
by the truckloads
to join campaign or protest rallies.
Some of them bought bikes
with the agricultural loans
sanctioned to them
and roamed around
as petty contractors
or as musclemen
of the tender-fixing mafia.

The farmland went
bald and barren;
the barnyard looked bare
the groves and orchards
lost their greenery
the vagaries of the weather
made the river
mostly remain dry
and at times
burst into a fury.
We never knew
when the village
that had once kept us
in a warm tight hug
loosened its hold
and lost its glory.

Perhaps we swam
against the current
and went farther
and farther away.

☐☐

A Portrait of the Twenty-First Century

One day
when I was busy
painting a portrait
of the twenty-first century,
I was distracted
by someone's footsteps
behind me.
I looked back and saw
a beautiful young girl
with collyrium in her eyes,
alta on her feet
and her forehead
marked with sandalwood paste,
smiling at me.

Then she disappeared
amidst the joyous laughter
of a group of girls
merrily playing on the swings.

She went away
breathing new life
into a bunch of old memories
I had long taken for dead,

memories of the pubescent earth
bathing in the early monsoon drizzle;
the backyard of every home
in the village
throbbing with a flurry of activities
and the loud laughter
of frolicsome women.

The mangroves, the river banks
and the village playground
pulsating with
youngmen playing kabaddi
and the big banyan tree
at the centre of the village
echoing with roaring commands
of elderly men
busy at a game
of dice or cards;
and all that followed by
community lunches and dinners
with the speciality
of chicken broth or mutton fry.

The memories
of the *Raja* Festival
in each of my youthful years –
watching the open-air opera
on the village ground
on a moonlit night
in the company
of my childhood friends,
or going across the river
in a country ferry boat

to visit near and dear ones
in the neighbouring villages,
and the seemingly endless
bonhomie among the village folks –
now look like mirages
in the distant horizon.

And the charmingly
bucolic lyricism of the songs
of village maidens on the swings
echoing in the air,
and the picture of pristine purity
and innocence of lilfe
mirrored in their smiles
still gleam in my consciousness
like the gilt-edged pages
of a glorious history.

This evening
they are going
to recreate the *Raja* spirit
with lots of fanfare
within the confines of
the gaudily decorated concrete walls
of the city centre.

Learned guest-speakers
will shed gallons of
crocodile tears
over the loss of
the old-world charms
of an idyllic utopia
followed by a session of

poetry recitation
where poets after poets
will mourn the loss of innocence
through their parodic elegies.

And finally
the deejay of the orchestra
with his digital acoustics
will take over,
drowning everything
in the cacophonous din
of western pop beats;
and the roving glare
of the laser beams
will sweep away
the foundations
of a centuries-old civilization
to celebrate the macabre face
of a mercantile culture.

❒❒

Under the Shade of a Fruit-bearing Tree

He wished everybody well
and thus earned
a place for himself
in their hearts;
and we who are
related to him by blood
are fortunate
to carry in ourselves
a spark of his purest soul.

His blessings come to us
flying across rivers, mountains
and even borders
when we wish him
on his birthday
every new year;
and they come to us
like a fresh sea wave
inundating the parched shores.

Our shared moments
in the past
remind us of
his reassuring presence;
he was always there

to lend a helping hand
to whoever needed help;
he would bring out
from his drawer
a small notebook
with phone numbers
and calmly breathe
a few sweet words
in to the mouthpiece of his phone –
Lo and see !
your work is done.

He told us tales –
and he had so many to tell –
real-life episodes and anecdotes
all culled from his long experience
with people and in places
near and far;
tales good enough
to calm our jangled nerves
and to show us the light
at the end of the tunnel.

Like good poetry
flowing from a pure heart
the endless stream
of his heart-felt empathy
with his fellow human beings
has saturated
so many souls.

Unflappable, he ventured out
into the sea

against all odds
and like an able helmsman
safely steered through
the turbulent waters of time.

Like a small sapling
that grows into
a big fruit-bearing tree
providing food and shelter
to the birds on its branches
and to the passersby
under its shade,
he grew in stature
to be our moral anchor
and the source of
our spiritual sustenance.

Blessed am I
to be bound by kinship
to such a great soul;
and this day
I wish and pray
he lives for
a hundred years more
for the world now needs
such souls
more than ever before.

◻◻

(Upon the ninetieth birthday of my beloved maternal uncle, Justice (Rtd.) Prafulla Kishore Mohanty)

The Parting Moment

When an active life
spanning over long years
came to an end
and they gathered
to bid me goodbye
and perhaps to consign
me to history,
albeit with all their goodwill,
it did not matter
how history would
look upon that life –
but if it would ever record
its humble beginnings,
the strifes and struggles
it went through,
the string of disappointments
occasionally punctuated
by small joys –
all that would
remain in my heart
written in stone
like the lithic inscriptions
on the walls of
ancient caves and temples.

It would not be easy
to forget
the shared tears and smiles
the camaraderie of colleagues
and their collective aspirations –
not easy for
a Vishu Moharana[7]
to keep away
from the Konark
of his blood and sweat
while it was still incomplete.

But the old had to
give way to the new
and the new generation
bubbling with energy
and backed by expertise
was ready to take over;
they too were there
with their bouquets
of best wishes
and affectionate gifts.
No amount of poetry
would have been
enough for the moment
and one could
only wish them well in return
and pray for their success.

---

7   *The legendary Odia sculptor and architect who headed a team of 1200 Craftsmen to build the famous Sun Temple at Konark in Puri in the twelfth Century.*

And hereafter
whenever I visit this place
I will find myself at home
as naturally as the raindrops
find their homes
in ponds and lakes
and just as effortlessly
as a prodigal son
finds his way back home.

Let this going away
and coming back continue;
let there be the promise
of reunion
in the poignancy
of this parting moment
till the boatman
ferrying across the banks
finally falls asleep
amidst the tearful farewell
of his loved ones.

□□

[Upon my superannuation]

The Forgotten Destination

He always looked
in a hurry to leave;
not knowing much
about his destination,
we thought he had
some important appointments
to keep.

Then one day
he gave us the slip
and suddenly went away
leaving us all stunned;
we had no idea
that was the destination
he was planning for
so long.

His poetry sprouted
in the rustic soil
of his village
and like a luxuriant creeper
spread its tendrils
all around
to finally find itself
in full bloom
in the steel city of Rourkela.

He was a soul
in search of the truth;
like an accomplished potter,
he gave the same clay
different shapes and colours
to reach perfection.

He perhaps had
a presage of the things to come
for he was in a hurry
to finish all his pending jobs –
his children's education,
wife's surgery –
got a house built for them
and furnished it
with furniture
of reasonable cost
but of good taste
got a few collections published
personally proof-reading the manuscripts
attended the book-launch events
with the fervour
of a beginner.

And then suddenly
one evening we heard
he was in the I.C.U.
of the Ispat General Hospital.

And at that moment
he perhaps had
a vision of his
ailing mother's face

he had not seen
for a long time,
a glimpse of his
long lost birth place;
perhaps he remembered
his sister-in-law's complaint
that he had forgotten her
and the unspoken one
of his beloved sister's
parting look-
perhaps he wished
to visit them all
one last time.

The crowd at the hospital corridor
grew bigger and bigger
as more and more
friends, well-wishers,
colleagues and lovers
of his poetry
came rushing
to join his anxious wife and children.
But he quietly
gave them the slip
at the dead of the night.

Those of us
who knew him well
had thought that
he was planning
to go on a long sabbatical
but never thought
that he would leave

so suddenly
and for such a destination.

And we were left
wondering why
when the long night
of his struggles
was about to end,
he turned away
from the daybreak
and why
his vibrant, living face
was snatched away from us
only to be etched
on the pages of an album
or on the dust-jackets
of his posthumously published poetry collections.

□□

[Upon the untimely death of the poet, Sanat Ray, who was like a younger brother to me.]

A Different Place :
A Different Awakening

There was no big banyan tree around
under whose shade
they could have gathered
to spend a few
leisure hours
in the afternoon
after a hard day's work
gossiping, and in the course,
perhaps stumbling
upon some great ideas.

So they chose
the shade of a small *amla* tree
that could hardly
provide any shade
and amidst the twittering
of a few birds
on its branches
a bunch of good-hearted
fresh recruits of the steel plant
flocked together
in the evening
talking about matters
near and far.

A makeshift tea stall
soon came up nearby
to cater to their needs;
and one evening
while sipping tea and chatting,
someone came up
with the idea
of finding a permanent shade
where they could
get into a huddle
in the evening,
exchange ideas,
read out poetry
written by themselves,
comment on them
and thereby try to
understand themselves
and the world.

They unanimously
chose an open space
not far from where they gathered
raised a humble
brick-walled asbestos shade
that heralded an era
of creativity
in the steel city.

And those who had
left their poverty-ridden homeland
in search of a better life,
like flocks of storm-beaten birds
looking for a habitat,

soon found their soulmates
in an unknown land
and stood in solidarity
with one another.

The city clad in
dust and smoke
that had once seemed
so alien to them
now looked their own.

They went about
reordering, recreating their lives
not in vacuous imagination
but in dealing with
the blood and sweat
of so many
of the toiling masses.

And for more than
half a century ever since
the voice of righteous protest
they raised
through their poetry
has echoed around
spreading the message of hope
among the have-nots
and serving notices
to their tormentors.

□□

[Upon the golden jubilee celebrations of the Cultural Academy, Rourkela.]

Black Eagle Books

www.blackeaglebooks.org
info@blackeaglebooks.org

Black Eagle Books, an independent publisher, was founded as a nonprofit organization in April, 2019. It is our mission to connect and engage the Indian diaspora and the world at large with the best of works of world literature published on a collaborative platform, with special emphasis on foregrounding Contemporary Classics and New Writing.

www.ingramcontent.com/pod-product-compliance
Lightning Source LLC
Chambersburg PA
CBHW020545080526
44583CB00013B/1000